TRUTH or BUSTED

WARM GLADIATOR BLOOD WAS USED AS MEDICINE

The fact or fiction behind ROMANS

Peter Hepplewhite

WAYLAND

First published in 2014 by Wayland

Copyright © Wayland 2014

Wayland
338 Euston Road
London NW1 3BH

Wayland Australia
Level 17/207 Kent Street
Sydney, NSW 2000

Editor: Elizabeth Brent
Design: Rocket Design (East Anglia) Ltd
Illustration: Alex Paterson

A catalogue record for this book is available from the British Library.
ISBN: 978 0 7502 8134 8
eBook ISBN: 978 0 7502 9346 4
Lib eBook ISBN: 978 0 7502 8730 2
Dewey Number: 937-dc23

Printed in China
10 9 8 7 6 5 4 3 2 1

Wayland is a division of Hachette Children's Books,
an Hachette UK company
www.hachette.co.uk

All illustrations by Shutterstock, except 4, 8, 15, 24−25, 28, 34−35, 41, 48, 52, 64, 70−71, 78, 81, 84−85

eh?
WOW!
check it out!
Really?
ortle
I can't believe it!
PHEW!
tee-hee!
That's incredible!
You're pulling my leg
No way!
COR!
FREAKY!
ell, I ver!
It's Amazing!
Awesome!

PREPARE
TO BE
ROCKED

BY THE
ANCIENT
ROMANS

read on!

Read this bit first...!

From around 300 BCE to 300 CE, the Romans were the most powerful people in the world. They occupied 5 million square kilometres of the globe, ruled over about a quarter of the world's population and still found time to invent aqueducts, concrete, newspapers, roads AND the calendar we still use today. Phew! To put you in the picture, read on for a whistle-stop tour through Roman history.

The centre of the Roman Empire was the vast, buzzy city of Rome. According to Roman legend, Rome was founded by (and named after) Romulus — a warrior who had been raised by a she-wolf, but was the son of the god Mars. Modern historians have already busted this myth though — the first Romans were actually farmers — which is a pity, because the half-god-raised-by-she-wolf makes a MUCH better story.

Around 500 BCE, the Roman farmers decided they'd had enough of their king, Tarquin the Proud, so they got rid of him and began ruling themselves instead, as a republic. The Republic lasted for almost 500 years, and became an empire in 30 BCE. The Empire reached its peak in 117 CE, at which point it incorporated 40 countries throughout Europe, North Africa and the Middle East, before crumbling altogether in 476 CE when the final Roman emperor was forced to retire.

If you love history, you'll be riveted by the Romans. Come on, who wouldn't want to know if...

☆ *The Latin language was rich — in insults?*

☆ *Emperor Caligula was nicknamed Bootikins by his soldiers?*

☆ *A Roman soldier's best friend was his mule?*

Truth or Busted: Warm Gladiator Blood Was Used as Medicine gets to the truth about these, and many, many more ridiculous Roman 'facts'. Killer tortoises? You'll find them here. Wacky wizards? We've got 'em. Blood-sucking fish? Check. So if this sounds like your kind of thing, turn the page to discover the truth about the epic, the enormous, the en-credible Roman Empire...

read on!

Roman timeline

Confused about what happened when, and where? Here at Truth or Busted Headquarters we've produced this handy timeline to help you out!

753 BCE	The city of Rome is founded
753-509 BCE	Rome is ruled by kings
509 BCE	Rome becomes a republic
200 BCE	Rome rules over all of Italy
246 BCE	The first gladiators fight to the death
264-146 BCE	Rome fights three wars with her greatest rival, the city of Carthage
146 BCE	Rome begins to annex territory outside Italy
27 BCE	Augustus becomes the first Roman emperor
73 BCE	A slave revolt, led by Spartacus, shakes Rome
53 BCE	The Parthians wipe out a Roman army in Syria

44 BCE	Julius Caesar is assassinated
43 CE	The Romans invade Britain during the reign of Emperor Claudius
79 CE	Mount Vesuvius erupts, burying the cities of Pompeii and Herculaneum
117 CE	The Roman Empire reaches its greatest size under Emperor Trajan
122 CE	Emperor Hadrian inspects his new frontier wall in Britain
165–180 CE	The Antonine plague kills about a third of all Romans
313 CE	Emperor Constantine ends the persecution of Christians
410 CE	The Roman army leaves Britain
480 CE	The last Roman emperor, Julius Nepos, dies

The Latin language was full of insults

Ancient Rome was a rough city and in the packed and jostling streets, tempers could easily fray.
But did the Romans really insult each other in LATIN??

Derideo te caudix!

Caveat nugator!

And the truth is...

Well, yes. Latin was the language spoken by the people of Rome — even if they were yelling at one another — and it became the official language of the Roman Empire. Here's a crash course in rude Latin:

Asine! .... Donkey!

Caenum! .... Filth!

Caveat! .... Watch it!

Derideo te! .... I laugh at you!

Spurcifer! .... Scum bucket! (Literally 'bearer-of-filth')

Tace! .... Shut up!

Fugitive! .... Jailbait or escaped slave

Malum! .... Bad thing! (Like 'idiot')

Obesus porcus! .... Fat pig!

Ructabunde! .... Gas bag!
(Literally 'full of burps' or 'big burper')

Stulte! .... Idiot!

Vapula! .... Go hang yourself!

Cucurbita! .... You pumpkin!

Nebulo! .... Trash!

Fatue! .... Fool!

Caudix! .... You blockhead!

Nugator! .... Pipsqueak!

Stolide! .... Dummy!

Vappa! .... Scum!

Verdict: _____

9

GOOD GOD!

Are you baffled by Bacchus? Mystified by Minerva? Worry not! Follow our bit-by-bit guide to some members of the Holy Roman Family:

SATURN

Also known as 'Old Father Time', Saturn was the Roman god of... time (no prizes for guessing that one). He ruled the gods before Jupiter, and was the father of Jupiter, Neptune and Pluto. Every year in mid-December, the Romans held a festival in honour of Saturn called Saturnalia, which lasted for seven days. During Saturnalia, slaves had a treat. They dressed in fine clothes, sat at the head of the table and were served at a banquet by their masters.

PSSST! You may notice a certain similarity between the names of the Roman gods and the planets in our Solar System. This is no coincidence – the Romans named the bright objects they could see in the night sky after their gods – a tradition that continues today.

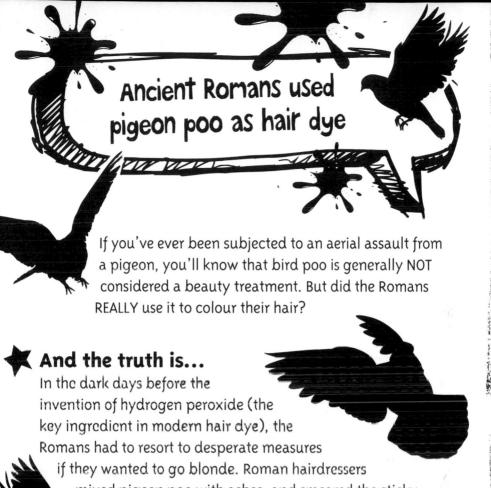

Ancient Romans used pigeon poo as hair dye

If you've ever been subjected to an aerial assault from a pigeon, you'll know that bird poo is generally NOT considered a beauty treatment. But did the Romans REALLY use it to colour their hair?

★ And the truth is...

In the dark days before the invention of hydrogen peroxide (the key ingredient in modern hair dye), the Romans had to resort to desperate measures if they wanted to go blonde. Roman hairdressers mixed pigeon poo with ashes, and smeared the sticky concoction all over their clients' hair. It gets worse. To complete the dying process, the poo-and-ash mixture had to be rinsed from the hair with... urine. Both the pee and the poo contained a chemical called ammonia, which lightens hair. Waste not, want not...

Verdict: (a yucky)  TRUTH

11

The Roman Empire was run by 40,000 men

If we know one thing about the Roman Empire, it's that it was ENORMOUS. And an organisation that size would have needed lots of people to run it, right? But 40,000 men?! Surely that's about 39,000 too many?

 And the truth is...

To put things in perspective, let's first have a look at a snapshot of the Roman Empire in 117 CE:

Emperor: Trajan

Size: 5 million square kilometres (3 million square miles)

Included: Western Europe, North Africa and the Middle East (around 40 modern countries)

Population: 88 million

Army: About 350,000 men, including 25 legions*

All of this was run by a ruling class called the *honestiores* — meaning 'the more honourable ones' — made up of... 40,000 adult men (about 0.1% of the population).

The honestiores came in three sorts:

Senators or patricians
The very top people, who held most of the political power in Rome.

Equestrians or knights
They served as officers in the army and as officials who ran the Empire.

Decurians
wealthy citizens who ran towns across the Empire.

And with all that power came some great perks. If honestiores broke the law they couldn't be tortured, crucified, sent to the mines or thrown to wild beasts, unlike the average Roman citizen.

The rest of the population, the 99.9%, were called — wait for it — *humiliores*. Now what could that mean? Yep, you guessed It, 'lesser beings' or 'the humble ones'.

Verdict:  TRUTH

A legion was an elite Roman fighting force, about 5,000-men strong. To find out more about Roman soldiers, turn to page 30.

Julius Caesar was murdered at a bus stop

Gaius Julius Caesar (100–44 BCE) was arguably the greatest Roman general ever. So why was he murdered? And, more to the point, what was he doing at a bus stop?

 ## And the truth is...

Caesar became too powerful for his own good. After beating his rival Pompey in a civil war, Caesar made himself dictator for life. To show how great he was, and to annoy his enemies, he sat on an ivory throne and wore purple robes, the colour of the old kings of Rome.

This was too much for those senators who wanted Rome to remain a republic. On the Ides of March (15 March) 44 BCE, about 60 conspirators led by Marcus Brutus and Gaius Cassius struck. They surrounded Caesar and stabbed him to death.

Caesar was assassinated at the bottom of a flight of steps in an area of the Senate known as the Curia of Pompeii. In 2012, archaeologists found the spot — next to a present-day bus and tram stop called *Torre Argentina*.

Verdict: **BUSTED**

PSSST! Caesar got his revenge on the senators. His nephew Octavian became the first Roman emperor, taking the name Augustus. But the senators Brutus and Cassius weren't cowardly assassins. They raised an army and fought bravely against Octavian at the Battle of Philippi in 42 BCE.

All Roman emperors were evil

The early Roman emperors all came from two powerful noble families, the Julians and the Claudians. When one or two families rule a country or an empire, this is called a dynasty, rather like the Tudors in English history. But were these emperors good, bad or just plain mad?

★ And the truth is...

Julio-Claudian Dynasty 27 BCE–68 CE		
Emperor	Reputation	Good, bad or mad
Augustus	First emperor, ended years of civil war	Good
Tiberius	Liked throwing people off cliff tops from his villa in Capri	Good at the beginning, then both bad AND mad
Caligula	Made his horse Incitatus a senator	Mad as a hatter
Claudius	Emperor who conquered Britain	Good, but weak
Nero	Poisoned his rival Britannicus at the dinner table	Bad (mostly)

After Augustus, the Julio-Claudian dynasty was a disaster.

Or was it?

It's likely these emperors were pretty bad, though most of what we know about them comes from accounts written by ancient historians like Tacitus, Suetonius and Dio. They wrote years after the events and used gossip and rumour to make good stories.

Verdict:  TRUTH (probably)

KEEP IT IN THE FAMILY!

None of the Julio-Claudian emperors were succeeded by their sons.

Augustus was the great-nephew of Julius Caesar.

Tiberius was Augustus's stepson.

Caligula was the great-nephew of Tiberius.

Claudius was the great-nephew of Augustus and the nephew of Tiberius.

Nero was the great-nephew and adopted son of Claudius.

The Romans feared a 'parting shot'

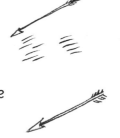

I'll bet you've faced a parting shot — that annoying name someone calls you as they disappear round a corner, so you don't have time to react…? But why would fearsome warriors like the Romans fear such a thing?

 And the truth is…

In 53 BCE, a Roman general, Crassus, came a cropper in the province of Syria, in modern Turkey. His mistake? He invaded the Parthian Empire.

The Roman army had never met anything like the Parthians. At the Battle of Carrhae, Parthian horse archers destroyed seven legions — killing 20,000 men, including Crassus, and taking 10,000 prisoners. The archers were kept supplied with arrows by camel trains.

The Parthians were such skilled horsemen that they even fired arrows while they were riding away, turning backwards in their saddles. The Romans called this a Parthian shot — the origin of the modern phrase 'a parting shot'.

Verdict:

The Romans invaded Britain for the hunting dogs

The Romans LOVED to hunt, and they paid good money for British hunting dogs (which looked a bit like Irish wolfhounds). Now, we all love our pet dogs, but was this a reason to invade?

 And the truth is...

Julius Caesar raided, but couldn't conquer, Britain in 55 BCE. So the Romans reckoned they had unfinished business there.

The geographer, philosopher and historian Strabo reported that the Romans traded with the British, so knew Britain was rich in grain, gold, silver, iron, animal hides, slaves — and those dogs. All that treasure, just begging to be conquered!

Enter the new, and vulnerable, emperor, Claudius. He had paid out a fortune to the army (200 million *denarii*, or about £2.4 billion) to stay in power and needed loot — and a quick victory to show he was tough. In the summer of 43 CE, an army of 40,000 Roman soldiers, led by General Aulus Plautius, landed on the beaches of Kent.

Verdict: A little bit **TRUTH** but mainly **BUSTED**

Emperor Caligula was nicknamed 'Bootikins'

Caligula's real name was *Gaius Julius Caesar Germanicus*. So why did everyone call him Caligula? What did HE think about that? And what does Caligula even mean?

 And the truth is...

Caligula was the son of the popular general, Germanicus, who led the armies of the Rhine. He lived with his father on campaign in Germany and became a mascot for the army.

When he was two years old, he came on parade in miniature armour and army boots, or *caliga*, so the soldiers nicknamed him *Caligula*, meaning 'Little Boots' or 'Bootikins'.

Caligae were army-issue marching sandals, and they were excellent. They were strong, well-ventilated and had metal studs on the soles to make them last longer. There were definitely worse names Caligula could have been called.

But just think about it. The most powerful man in the world being called... Bootikins. Caligula HATED the nickname — and can you blame him?

Verdict:

caligula

Having read on p17 that Caligula made his horse a senator, you probably already have an inkling that this Roman rotter wasn't the sanest of men. The senator horse, however, was just the tip of the iceberg. Caligula was REALLY bonkers. Here are a few examples of his wacky behaviour:

- He was fond of dressing up, and appeared in public dressed as the goddess Venus, the military leader Alexander the Great, and the Greek hero Hercules, among others.

- He had a temple built with a life-size gold statue of himself at its centre. Every day, the statue's clothes were changed to match what Caligula was wearing.

- During an attempt to invade Britain in 40 CE, Caligula lined his troops up on a beach in modern-day France, and ordered them to attack the sea. They then gathered seashells to send back to Rome as 'treasure'.

- Shocked at the price of wild animal feed, Caligula had the beasts destined for the gladiatorial arena fed on... criminals.

The Romans didn't put up with such bizarre behaviour for long. Caligula was stabbed to death by one of his guards at the age of just 29.

Emperor Nero burned down Rome because he wanted a new palace

Nero murdered his mother, and some say he killed his wife too. Did this evil emperor also burn down Rome?!

In 64 CE, on the night of 19 July, a fire broke out in the shops lining the Circus Maximus, Rome's giant chariot stadium. The flames raged for nine days and when the smoke cleared, 10 of Rome's 14 districts were in ruins.

For almost 2,000 years a burning question has been asked about this ancient catastrophe. Was Nero so evil that he set fire to his own city?

★ And the truth is...

Roman historians, writing years after Nero's death, claimed that he ordered the burning of Rome to make space for a bigger palace. And worse, that he gleefully played the lyre (a kind of stringed instrument, like a small harp) while the flames soared.

But for once, Nero seems to have been Mr Nice Guy. When he heard the news of the inferno, the emperor rushed back to Rome from his country estates to take control.

Nero's Disaster Plan:

① Coordinate fire fighting.

② Open palace grounds to the homeless.

③ Ship in food to prevent mass starvation.

④ New fire regulations: wider streets; space houses out; build in brick.

Pretty good then, so what about the accusations? Was Nero the greatest arsonist in history?

After the fire, Nero did build a vast new palace called the Domus Aurea (or Golden House) right in the heart of Rome. So was the fire started deliberately by a wicked emperor — or was it just a coincidence?

The verdict is uncertain, but most historians believe Nero didn't burn Rome deliberately, he just took advantage of a tragic accident. Nero himself blamed Christians for the fire. The ancient historian Tacitus writes that a multitude were rounded up and crucified, torn apart by dogs or set on fire and used as night lights. No more Mr Nice Guy!

Verdict: (a shaky) **BUSTED**

The Romans built a wall to keep out the Scots

The Romans — tough, brave, fierce warriors though they were — were TERRIFIED of the Scots, a tribe of bloodthirsty barbarians living in modern Scotland. But did they really go so far as to build a wall to keep the Scots out? And was a wall any use against a load of bloodthirsty barbarians anyway?

And the truth is...

The Romans did indeed build a wall to protect themselves from the Scots, but it wasn't just any old wall. It was a Very Special Wall indeed. It was largely planned and built by three Roman legions, the II (Second), VI (Sixth) and XX (Twentieth). Surveying and building the wall took 12 years. It was 118 kilometres long, 4–5 metres high and up to 2–3 metres thick. There were signal towers every half a kilometre, and a small fort for about 30 men every one-and-a-half kilometres.

When Emperor Hadrian visited Britain in 122 CE, he inspected the new northern frontier. The mighty wall ran from the River Tyne in the east to the Solway Firth in the west. Parts of it still stand today, and are known as Hadrian's Wall.

Verdict: TRUTH

Boils brought down the Roman Empire

The Romans faced many enemies over the centuries, but their deadliest foes were too small to see — germs. Soldiers fighting in the Middle East came home with boils, diarrhoea and fevers. Before long, people throughout the Empire were dropping like flies with the same symptoms. What on Earth was going on?

★ And the truth is...

Between 165–180 CE, a plague raged through the Roman Empire, killing more than a third of the population. In 178 CE, the outbreak was so ferocious that 2,000 people a DAY were dying in Rome alone. Marcus Aurelius Antoninus Augustus was emperor when the plague hit and it lasted throughout his reign. He was unlucky enough to have the disease named after him — the Antonine Plague. A top Roman doctor, Galen, described the terrible symptoms: fever, diarrhoea and pustules — small, blood-filled boils all over the skin. Modern doctors have read Galen's diagnosis, and are pretty sure the plague was smallpox.

Verdict:  TRUTH

Galen

Top Roman doctor Galen learned his medical skills stitching wounded gladiators back together. In the process, he made some pretty impressive anatomical discoveries, too, including:

 Urine is formed in the kidneys

 Arteries carry blood

 The larynx is the source of people's voices

Galen was born in Turkey to Greek parents, but moved to Rome to work. He was the personal physician of not one, not two, but THREE Roman emperors (they kept dying, which doesn't say a lot about his healing abilities...). Galen compiled all the Roman and Greek medical knowledge of the time, whilst adding some theories of his own to the mix. His influence over the field of medicine reigned supreme for 1,500 years after his death – it wasn't until the Renaissance period, in the 14th century CE, that people began to question his ideas.

A Roman soldier's best friend was his mule

Roman soldiers were nicknamed 'Marius's Mules' after General Gaius Marius. In 107 BCE, he brought in sweeping changes to make the Roman army a professional fighting force. But why the nickname? And were Roman soldiers REALLY best friends with their mules?!

★ And the truth is...

The finest Roman troops served in the legions — elite, 5,000-men squads. Legionaries were infantry (foot soldiers) but they could move fast — marching up to 50 kilometres a day. To keep up this speed, Marius scrapped the legions' baggage trains — convoys of slow-moving wagons that carried supplies.

Instead each man had to carry his own equipment, armour, weapons, and a week's rations in huge packs on his back. All this weighed about 30–35 kilograms. To civilians, they looked like loaded mules — hence Marius's Mules! Just as well then that each squad had two real mules to help out. They carried the heaviest kit, like leather tents, iron cooking pots, spits for roasting meat and grindstones for making flour. And in emergencies, the troops could eat them!

Verdict: _____ (a grateful) **TRUTH** ___

Rampaging Romans — Mess Mates

Recruits served for up to 25 years and the army became like a family. They lived in eight-man squads called *contubernia* and shared a barrack room or a tent on campaign. Squads ate, slept, trained and fought together. Soldiers called one another *contubernalis*, meaning tent-mate or mess-mate. The basic unit of the modern British army is the 'section' – eight men led by a corporal. Wonder where they got that idea from?

GOOD GOD!

Are you baffled by Bacchus? Mystified by Minerva? Worry not! Follow our bit-by-bit guide to some members of the Holy Roman Family:

I'll just run that past the wife...

JUPITER

The son of Saturn, and the king of the gods. The thunderbolt was Jupiter's weapon, and his messenger was the eagle. The Romans believed that he looked after them and their city. All the other gods were frightened of Jupiter, but he was scared of no-one, except perhaps...

JUNO

Jupiter's wife, and the queen of the gods. Juno was the goddess of marriage and of women, and her bird was the peacock. Juno was the mother of Mars and Vulcan (see p47).

The Roman army used Special Forces

The name's Bondus, James Bondus.

Roman legions were tough and could turn their hand to anything. But did even they sometimes need specialist help on the battlefield?

⭐ And the truth is...

The legions were supported by back-up troops called 'auxiliaries'. In Latin, *auxilia* means help. Auxiliaries were recruited from warrior peoples on the frontiers of the Empire.

The best Roman archers came from Crete and Syria, while Numidian cavalry came from the nomadic tribes who roamed the Sahara desert. They rode small, fast horses, ideal for hit-and-run attacks. Slingers came from the Balearic Islands off the coast of Spain. They used strips of leather to hurl stones with deadly accuracy, ideal for sneaky ambushes.

Verdict:

31

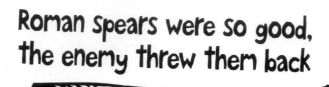

Roman spears were so good, the enemy threw them back

So, you're in a battle. An enemy throws a spear and it lands next to you. What are you going to do?

A. Pick it up and run away?
B. Smash it?
C. Throw it back?

You'd throw it back, wouldn't you, hoping to hit an enemy or two? Did the Roman army's opponents do the same?

 And the truth is...

The Roman javelin, or *pilum*, was a two-metre-long wooden shaft, with a barbed iron head for piercing armour. It could be used in hand-to-hand combat but was usually thrown, and had a maximum range of about 30 metres (about 100 feet).

The pilum was designed to bend on impact so that it couldn't be thrown back. Even better, if the head stuck in an enemy shield and then bent, it made the shield useless.

Verdict: **BUSTED**

Roman spears were so good the enemy COULDN'T throw them back!

Marcus Antonius

If you've ever read, or seen, the Shakespeare play Antony and Cleopatra, you'll know all about Marcus Antonius – the lovesick Roman warrior who, besotted with the Egyptian pharaoh Cleopatra, forfeits his power and his life. Or do you? The true-life Marcus Antonius was VERY different from Shakespeare's foolish hero – he was a brilliant politician and general who played a key role in the transformation of Rome from a republic to an empire.

Antonius served as a military commander under Julius Caesar. Following Caesar's assassination (see pp14–15 for more on this sorry tale), he avenged his death by forming an allegiance with another of Caesar's generals and his adopted son, Octavian, and defeating the murderers. The three men ruled Rome together for a while, but in 31 BCE, disagreements between Octavian and Antonius escalated into full-blown civil war. Antonius was defeated, and fled to Egypt with Cleopatra, where he committed suicide.

The Romans used tortoises in battle

Have you ever heard of the Roman war tortoise? Slow-moving but unstoppable!

Chaaaaaarge.

And the truth is...

Well-trained Roman units could drop into the *testudo* — or tortoise — formation in seconds. The soldiers at the front and sides held their shields tightly together to make a wall. The troops in the rear ranks rested their shields on their helmets to make a protective shell. The testudo was so strong that a chariot could be driven across the top of it.

But no animals were harmed in the making of a testudo.

Verdict: TRUH

> # The most feared Roman weapon was a wild ass

An ass is another name for a donkey. Were the Romans using weird animals on the battlefield again?

 And the truth is...

The Roman army had artillery — catapults that fired a range of devastating missiles. The most fearsome Roman catapult was called the *onager*, Latin for 'wild ass', because of the way it kicked when it was fired.

The onager had a long arm fastened with thick, twisted ropes that acted like springs. Soldiers called *ballistarii* pulled back the arm with a winch, twisting the ropes tighter. When the arm was released it shot forwards, smacked against a crossbar — and fired large rocks.

Verdict: —— **BUSTED** ——

Traffic kept the Romans awake at night

Do noisy neighbours ever keep you from sleeping?
Then pity the Ancient Romans — they lived in a 24-hour city!

 And the truth is...

Rome was by far the largest city in the ancient world. In the 2nd century CE, when Roman London had a population of about 60,000, over a million people lived in Rome.

The streets were so busy during the day that deliveries were banned. As soon as darkness fell, hundreds of wagons and their shouting drivers rumbled over the cobbled streets. The noise was so bad that the poet Juvenal penned a famous complaint:

Show me the apartment
that lets you sleep!

The wagons thundering past
through narrow twisting streets,

the oaths of drivers caught
in a traffic-jam, would rouse a dozing seal

— or an emperor.

Verdict:

Ancient Romans lived in high-rise flats

Rome was a city of splendid public buildings: the Colosseum (for games), the Forum (market place) and the Circus Maximus (for chariot races). But what about buildings for ordinary people? Where did THEY live?

⭐ And the truth is...

Most Romans lived in apartment blocks called *insulae*. By the 4th century there were 46,000 tenements and just 2,000 single-storey family homes. Some blocks were six or seven stories high, with 200 steps up to the top apartments. There were shops and workshops on the ground floors.

The poorest people lived in ramshackle blocks, with families crowded into one room. Middle-class apartments could be luxurious, with a large hall leading to a kitchen, living room and bedrooms. Each floor had a loo and a rubbish chute.

Verdict: _____

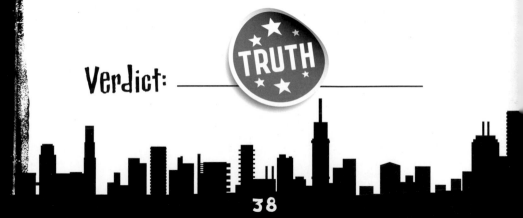

Rampaging Romans

The plagues of city life

Juvenal made a living from moaning in poems called Satires. Here's his list of the worst problems of life in Ancient Rome:

⭐ The cost of rents is sky high.

⭐ Landlords don't care if their crumbling slums collapse.

⭐ The rich barge through the crowds, carried in litters by slaves.

⭐ Housewives hurl rubbish from upstairs windows - including full chamber pots.

⭐ Even if you lock your doors, burglars will break in.

Any of this sound familiar? Although hopefully you haven't been hit by a flying chamber pot this year.

Public baths were palaces for the people

The Roman emperors built magnificent palaces for themselves, but they weren't the greatest buildings in Rome. To impress the ordinary folk, they built something far more useful...

⭐ And the truth is...

The grandest monuments in Ancient Rome were vast public baths. Among the best were the baths of Diocletian. Opened in 306 CE, they covered almost 130,000 square metres and had facilities for about 3,000 people.

As good as any modern leisure centre, the facilities included a gymnasium, libraries, snack bars, a huge swimming pool and the rooms at the heart of every baths: the *frigidarium* (cold bath), the *tepidarium* (lukewarm bath) and the *calidarium* (hot bath).

Vast, vaulted roofs soared overhead and the walls and floors were lined with the finest marble. And, as Romans had come to expect, it was all free.

Verdict:  TRUTH

41

Romans went to the
public baths to get clean

Most Romans went to the baths every day to
scrub up. The routine went something like this:

Bathing Plan:

1. Get very hot and sweaty in a steam room to loosen the dirt on the skin.

2. Be smeared in olive oil by a friend or a slave.

3. Have the oil scraped off with a blunt metal blade called a strigil.

4. Wash down in a hot or warm bath.

5. Finish with a plunge into the cold pool.

So far, so very hygienic. But was it really just
an exercise in getting as clean as a whistle, or
was there another agenda going on?

★ And the truth is...

Getting clean was actually just an excuse to have fun. The baths were the centre of Roman social life.

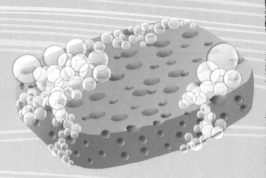

Pool Party Plan:

① Meet friends to bathe together and gossip.

② Exercise first, lift weights or play volleyball to work up an appetite.

③ Picnic time: open a flagon of wine and buy food from hawkers – fresh bread, chickpea soup, cooked sausages, mussels and cakes.

④ Finish with a game such as chess or tabula (like backgammon), lose a few denarii throwing dice.

Verdict: **BUSTED**

Roman police used astrology to catch criminals

Erm... ok. Astrology is the study of the stars and planets, and how they affect people, right? How is that any use in fighting crime?

⭐ And the truth is...

In 6 CE, the Emperor Augustus taxed the sale of slaves to pay for a combined force of police and fire fighters in Rome — the Vigils. There were seven divisions of Vigils, around 4,000 men led by the Praefectus Vigilum (The Chief Constable and Chief Fire Officer rolled into one) to keep a cap on crime. But how could they catch a culprit no one had seen?

In such cases, the Roman police turned to the stars for help. Books of astrology offered descriptions of criminals depending on the dominant planet in the heavens.

Verdict:  TRUTH

DOMINANT PLANET
SATURN

Suspect Description:

☆ Repulsive face

☆ Dark skinned

☆ Bloodshot, small eyes

☆ Slim and sickly looking

☆ Lots of body hair

☆ Bushy eyebrows

☆ A known liar

DOMINANT PLANET
MARS

Suspect Description:

☆ Red colour to skin

☆ Red hair

☆ Sharp eyed

☆ Life and soul of the
☆ party

☆ A master of jokes

DOMINANT PLANET
JUPITER

Suspect Description:

☆ Fat

☆ Big eyes

☆ Whites of the eyes small

☆ Beard rounded and curly

☆ Gentle personality

☆ Shouldn't cause trouble

Not a lot to go on, but better than nothing.

The Romans used spider webs as plasters

REALLY? We know healthcare was a bit primitive in ancient times, but using spider webs to heal wounds? Wouldn't a nice, clean bandage have been better?

And the truth is...

A nice, clean bandage probably would have been better, but these were in short supply in Ancient Rome. Plasters hadn't been invented yet, and cloth was expensive — too expensive to bleed on — so injured Romans turned to spider webs soaked in vinegar to help them heal. There was method in their madness though — modern scientists have discovered spider webs contain Vitamin K, which helps blood to clot.

Verdict: **TRUTH**

> **Pssst!** One wacky Roman emperor, Elagabalus (203–222 CE) used to COLLECT spider webs. Not to use as plasters, but simply because he could. It showed that he was SO important and powerful, he could afford to waste his time doing something as useless as collecting spider webs. Unsurprisingly, he didn't last long as emperor...

GOOD GOD!

Are you baffled by Bacchus? Mystified by Minerva? Worry not! Follow our bit-by-bit guide to some members of the Holy Roman Family:

MARS

The son of Jupiter and Juno (and supposedly the father of Romulus, see p5), Mars was the god of soldiers and of war. The month of March was named after Mars, because that was when soldiers began fighting again, after breaking for the winter months.

VULCAN

Also known as the blacksmith god, Vulcan was the god of fire and volcanoes, which are named after him. The Romans celebrated a festival in honour of Vulcan, called Vulcanalia, on 23 August each year, at the time when the summer heat meant their crops were in danger of catching fire. They lit bonfires and sacrificed small animals or live fish in the hope that Vulcan would spare the harvest.

Roman fathers could kill their own children

Good parents have to be strict sometimes. But suppose your Roman dad had the right to banish you from the family — or even kill you — if you misbehaved?

⭐ And the truth is...

The father was head of a Roman family — his title was the *paterfamilias*, and he had complete control over family affairs. A newborn baby was laid at its father's feet. If Dad picked the infant up, it became part of the family. If he refused, the poor kid had to go.

Unwanted babies were exposed (left outside to die of cold or thirst), or dumped at the nearest rubbish tip. (This was meant to be sort of kind — lots of people went to the rubbish tip). Anyone finding an abandoned baby could raise it as their own — or as a slave.

Children who defied their father could be sold as slaves or turned out of home until they did as they were told. Even adult children had to show respect, and anything they earned became the property of their father. Now you can imagine the arguments that caused...

Rampaging Romans — Baby Crisis!

Killing babies, or infanticide, was the only way poor Romans could control the size of their families. But with so many children dying naturally as well, the result was a Roman baby crisis! By the 4th century CE, the Emperor Constantine was worried. His thoughts ran like this: Not enough babies... so... not enough young men... so... not enough soldiers... so... no army... so... no Empire...

TO SAVE YOUNG LIVES HE TRIED TWO REFORMS:

* Baby-saving breakthrough 1:
  Give clothes and food to new parents if they keep their kids.

* Baby-saving breakthrough 2:
  Encourage parents to sell, rather than kill, their babies.

Verdict: ———————

Roman children used bones as toys!

We appreciate that the children of the Roman Empire had to fill the time before the invention of TVs, computers and games consoles somehow. But were bones really all they could find to play with?

 And the truth is...

A favourite Roman game, for children and adults alike, was 'Knucklebones', played with the anklebones of sheep and goats. Players tossed five small pieces of bone in the air, and then tried to catch as many as possible on the back of one hand. A variation of Knucklebones is still played today, but it's now called Jacks, and, to the relief of sheep and goats around the world, the pieces are made of metal or plastic.

Verdict:

GOOD GOD!

Are you baffled by Bacchus? Mystified by Minerva? Worry not! Here's a Truth or Busted guide to some members of the Holy Roman Family:

DIANA

The goddess of the hunt and the moon, and the daughter of Jupiter. She is often shown wearing a short, Greek-style tunic, and accompanied by a hunting dog. Diana was also the goddess of childbirth, and the twin sister of...

APOLLO

The god of the sun and light, Apollo was one of the most important Roman gods. The Romans believed that he drove a chariot pulled by flaming horses across the sky every day to light up the world.

Roman women had equal rights

Throughout history, it has often been an awful lot tougher to be a woman than to be a man. Was this the case in the Roman Empire?

And the truth is...

On the one hand, Roman women had far less freedom than men...

Girls were expected to honour and obey their fathers, marry early and then... honour and obey their husbands. Women couldn't vote or hold a public office (work for the government) and needed the permission of a male guardian to buy property (like a farm or a business) or make a will. Some marriages were unhappy and it was common for husbands to beat their wives.

On the other hand, Roman women could be independent...

Once a woman had three children, she had done her duty for Rome and earned the right to own property and make a will. Many marriages were happy, but if a husband was cruel a woman could go back to her father for protection — or get a divorce. Roman women, especially in poorer families, had jobs outside the home. They worked as shopkeepers, innkeepers, maids, laundresses, actresses and midwives. A wealthy few even became doctors, poets or painters.

Verdict: TRUTH for some, but mostly BUSTED

Emperor Augustus was ruled by his wife

Officially, women in Ancient Rome weren't allowed to hold political power. But did one Roman wife manage to bend the rules a little?

★ And the truth is...

Livia Drusilla became the first empress of Rome. She lived from 58 BCE to 29 CE and married Octavian, who later became Emperor Augustus (check him out on p16) in 38 BCE. But their romance was complicated... to say the least. When they first met, Livia was married and pregnant with her second child AND her father and her husband had fought against Octavian in two civil wars.

Even so, Octavian fell madly in love with Livia and was determined to marry her. (Remember Octavian was the most powerful man in Rome.) As a bonus, she came from the powerful Claudian family — a very useful connection. With his mind made up, it was time to leave his first wife, Scribonia.

On the day that Scribonia gave birth to their daughter Julia — he divorced her. Octavian then ordered Livia's husband, Tiberius Claudius Nero, to divorce her too — a not-so-subtle way of telling him he'd lost the war, so now he'd lost his wife. On 14 January, Livia's baby was born and she married Octavian on 17 January. Her ex-husband Tiberius gave her away at the ceremony — although he probably didn't have much choice. Octavian became the first Roman emperor, Augustus, in 27 BCE, and Livia was his most trusted adviser. They stayed married for over 50 years and Livia's son, Tiberius, became the next emperor.

read on!

There are some very dark rumours about Livia and poison... and murder. Livia and Augustus didn't have any children, so did Livia kill off anyone that got in the way of Tiberius (her son by her first husband) becoming Emperor?

Possible victims:

MARCELLUS Nephew of Augustus, died aged 19

GAIUS VIPSANIUS AGRIPPA Eldest son of Julia, daughter of Augustus. Died of an illness in 4 CE, aged 23

LUCIUS VIPSANIUS AGRIPPA second son of Julia. Died recovering from a wound in 2 CE, aged 19

AGRIPPA POSTUMUS third son of Julia. Executed by his guards in 14 CE, around the time Augustus died. Tiberius denied giving the order! So who did? Could it have been Livia?

AUGUSTUS Yes really. The emperor died after eating figs given to him by Livia — just as he was having doubts about Tiberius becoming his successor.

To be fair to Livia, some modern historians play down the murder angle and think the deaths were just coincidences. But others argue that there were rather a lot of those *coincidences*.

Verdict:  **TRUTH** (sort of)

Every new bride called her husband Gaius

Well that sounds confusing.
Suppose his real name
was Zethius? Or Polycarp?*
Where did Gaius come in?

 And the truth is...

Gaius was one of the commonest Roman names and thought to
be lucky. (10 Truth-or-Busted points if you can spot every Gaius
in this book).

At the wedding ceremony the bride would say *'Quando tu
Gaius, ego Gaia.'* Or, 'When and where you are Gaius, I then and
there am Gaia.' Try saying that quickly.

When they reached their new home, the bride rubbed fat on
the door posts and decorated them with wool. The best fat
came from a wolf — to frighten away evil spirits. The wool was a
symbol of prosperity. And just like today, the groom carried his
bride over the threshold — and it was very bad luck to drop her!

Verdict: ⎯⎯⎯ TRUTH ⎯⎯⎯

*Yep, those are real Roman names. As are Egnatius and Hilarius.

ROTTEN ROMANS

Emperor Nero

Emperor Nero was a Real Roman Rotter. His mother, Agrippina, plotted and schemed (and poisoned her husband, Emperor Claudius), to make sure that Nero became emperor. As a 'thank you', he had her murdered. In fact, having people murdered was something Nero did so often, it was practically a hobby. Here are some more unfortunate souls who met a sticky end on account of Nero:

* Britannicus was the son of Claudius, Nero's adoptive father and the previous emperor, and thus was a threat to Nero's rule. Nero decided to have Britannicus poisoned, but there was just one problem: a food taster tested all Britannicus' food and drink before he ate it, to make sure it wasn't poisoned. However, Nero had a plan. Some hot wine was prepared for Britannicus, and passed to the taster. The taster declared

it was safe, and gave the wine to Britannicus. Britannicus sipped the wine and complained it was too hot. Some cold water was added, Britannicus tried the wine again, and fell down dead. Nero had poisoned the water.

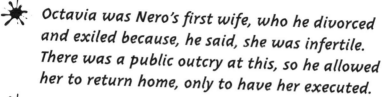 Octavia was Nero's first wife, who he divorced and exiled because, he said, she was infertile. There was a public outcry at this, so he allowed her to return home, only to have her executed.

Poppaea was Nero's second wife, and initially seemed to fare better than Octavia. However, it is alleged that Nero kicked her to death following an argument. If this is the case, he was certainly overcome with remorse, because his devastation at her untimely demise was well-documented.

In addition to members of his own family, Nero turned his murderous attentions to Christians. Nero HATED Christians, and came up with new and unpleasant ways to put them to death. This included tying them to posts, covering them in tar and setting them alight; dressing them in wild animal skins and throwing them to hoards of dogs; and crucifying them.

Romans snacked on stuffed dormice

EEEK!

Here at Truth or Busted HQ, we are aware that the Romans munched on some pretty weird stuff. Peacock? Sure. Fish-gut sauce? Er... yum. But DORMICE!? Surely that's a rodent too far?

And the truth is...

Stuffed dormouse was a favourite Roman recipe; however, before you puke in the corner, read on...

We are not talking about the little mice that invade your house. The Romans farmed and ate a species called the 'edible dormouse' or *glis glis*. When fattened up for eating, this could weigh around 300 grams.

A Roman cookbook from the late 4th century CE called the *Apicius* has this juicy recipe:

Stuff the dormice with minced pork as well as the flesh from all of the dormouse's limbs, together with ground pepper, pine nuts, laser and liquamen. Place them sewn up on a clay tile in the oven or cook them in a roasting pan.

Liquamen was a fermented fish sauce used in many Roman recipes, while laser was a very sharp spice.

Verdict: (A very scrummy) TRUTH

Rampaging Romans Freaky Food Fads

Roman gourmets queued up to eat an elephant's trunk. But why were they so keen on this nosy nosh? Well their thinking went... the trunk is close to the ivory tusks and ivory is worth a fortune... so the trunk must taste good.

Leeks became a fashionable food when Emperor Nero started eating them to improve his voice – all the better for singing along to his lyre (see page 22).

The *Apicius* has recipes for milk-fed snails cooked in olive oil, and flamingo boiled with water, salt, dill and a little vinegar.

Pepper was imported into the Roman Empire from India and cost a fortune. When Alaric the Visigoth was about to plunder Rome in 408 CE, he was paid off with gold, silver, silk and 3,000 pounds of pepper.

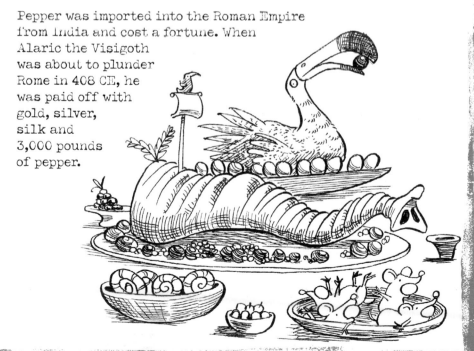

It was polite to puke at a party

By all accounts, Roman banquets were pretty messy... and the unfortunate slaves had to clean up afterwards. The philosopher Seneca describes the following delightful scene:

While we recline at a banquet, one slave wipes up the disgorged food (sick) while another crouches beneath the table to gather up the drunks' leftovers.

But would you really be a party pooper if you didn't puke during a Roman meal?

 And the truth is...

Seneca was a bit like a gossip blogger today. He was complaining about the outrageous behaviour of a few super-rich people who didn't care about ordinary manners. He had these people in mind when he wrote a much-quoted sentence:

Romans vomit so they may eat and eat so they may vomit.

But he didn't mean everyone, he was exaggerating to make a point. Many wealthy Romans held exotic banquets to impress their powerful friends. The wine flowed freely and guests were often drunk or sick — but most diners didn't vomit to make room for seconds.

Verdict: **BUSTED**

Rampaging Romans

Vomitorium

Did posh Romans have a special room to be sick in, called a vomitorium? The name seems to prove it – vomit means be sick, doesn't it? But names can sometimes be confusing!

A vomitorium was really a wide corridor in a public building like a theatre or amphitheatre, so-called because it enabled thousands of Romans to 'spew out' onto the streets in minutes.

The vomitoria of the Colosseum in Rome allowed 50,000 people to enter and exit their seats in 15 minutes, without anyone being trampled to death.

Roman baths were temples of hygiene

Roman baths were decorated with statues of Asclepius, the god of healing, and his daughter Hygeia, so this tells us the Romans reckoned they were healthy places. But how hygienic were they really...?

And the truth is...

Roman baths were actually pretty filthy.

Unlike modern pools, the water didn't circulate and there were no filters or disinfectants. What went into a Roman pool stayed there until it was emptied. So what could have lurked in the water?

Remember the olive-oil-and-strigil bit? (See page 42.) Not only did the bather wash off in the pool, the bath slaves swept the scrapings into the water.

Most baths had latrines, but some bathers didn't make it in time. I'm sure you can imagine the result...

Doctors advised the sick to take the baths, thus spreading their germs to the healthy. In the warm bathing rooms the bacteria must have had a party.

To cap it all, historians aren't certain how often the water was changed but the evidence suggests it was not all that much. Emperor Marcus Aurelius wrote:

What does bathing look like to you? Oil, nasty refuse, sludgy water, everything disgusting.

Verdict:

Romans preferred to poop in groups

Call us old-fashioned, but here at Truth or Busted HQ, we believe going to the bathroom is a strictly private activity. Was visiting a Roman loo a social occasion?

★ And the truth is...

According to a directory of buildings from the early 4th century, Rome had 144 public latrines or *foricae*. This was just as well. Remember those 46,000 apartment blocks? Most had no toilets, so Romans headed for the public loos in droves.

The latrines didn't have separate cubicles, so going to the loo meant sitting cheek-to-cheek with your friends and neighbours, chatting about politics and sport, or planning a dinner party. The best seats were marble benches with keyhole-shaped cut-outs. Underneath was a water channel, which continually flushed the waste into the city sewers.

Verdict: TRUTH

Private pooping was only for the rich

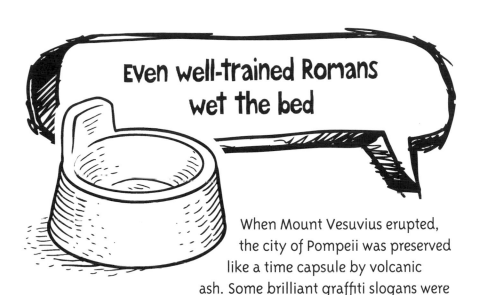

Even well-trained Romans wet the bed

When Mount Vesuvius erupted, the city of Pompeii was preserved like a time capsule by volcanic ash. Some brilliant graffiti slogans were scrawled on the walls, and one of the best reads:

We have wet the bed. I admit, we were wrong, my host.
If you ask 'why'?
There was no chamber pot.

This cheeky note was left for an innkeeper and reminds us of that essential Roman household appliance — a potty.

 And the truth is...

It's dark, it's raining and the public loos are half a mile away. So what does any sensible Roman do?

Every family had a potty or two for emergencies. Men used a *matella* (round pot) and women a *scaphium* (boat-shaped pot). Only lazy Romans wet the bed. In the morning they tipped the potties' contents into the street. Now you know Juvenal had real reasons for complaining (see page 39).

Verdict: — **BUSTED** —

The Romans had a postal delivery service

Roman postmen with bags of mail and red vans? Well, kind of…

 ## And the truth is…

Messages from the emperor, or Roman officials, were carried by the couriers of the *Cursus Publicus* — the Imperial postal service. Mounted postmen could travel around 80–100 kilometres a day with urgent messages for governors or army units. Official parcels or even people could travel more slowly on the system's freight vehicles: pack mules, wagons or boats.

Couriers changed horses at post houses every 15–25 kilometres and ate and slept at inns called *mansiones*. The mansiones were 30–50 kilometres apart and were like motorway service stations for the Roman road network. Local governors had to make sure facilities were up to scratch.

Verdict: _____ TRUTH _____

Roman roads always ran straight

Most Roman roads were built by the army to move troops quickly, and they soon became busy trade routes, packed with travellers and merchants. But were they always built in straight lines?

 And the truth is...

Yep, the Roman army liked to move quickly and the fastest way between two places is in a straight line. So how did the army manage to mark these out without modern technology?

The surveyors who decided the routes for Roman roads were called *grommatici*, after the main tool they used — a *groma*. This was a pair of wooden strips fastened together into a cross. Lines with weights were hung from each arm, and by lining up the weights with a pole 100 metres or so away, they got a straight line. In dense forest or hilly areas, the surveyors built fires and used the smoke as markers for the groma. The construction teams followed their directions.

But the Romans weren't stupid. If the planned route hit an obstacle — a steep hill, a marsh or a wide river — they zigzagged round it in short, straight lines.

Verdict: **TRUTH** and a bit **BUSTED**

Runaway Romans were forced to wear dog collars

Roman slaves had some rights. They couldn't be killed without good reason and they could complain to magistrates if they had been brutally treated. However, the word of a slave was not accepted in court unless he or she had been tortured first — to make sure they were telling the truth. What you might call a lose-lose situation. But were slaves really treated like dogs, and forced to wear collars if they ran away?

★ And the truth is...

Punishments were harsh, so slaves had to watch out for a master in a bad mood. Answering back or refusing to work brought swift penalties.

Run-of-the-mill treatment included days without food, wearing chains or being locked up in a cell. An angry owner might whip or brand a headstrong slave without anyone thinking this was over the top. Everyone agreed, slaves had to be taught humility.

Angry slaves rarely killed a cruel owner. The punishment was the death of EVERY slave in the household — whether they were involved or not.

The only way out was to escape. Runaways were called *fugitives* and the safest place to run to was their homeland — if they could reach it. The further from Roman authority, the better. Women with children had little hope of escaping.

Owners put up WANTED posters in public places, with full descriptions of fugitives and rewards for their capture. Some hired professional slave-catchers to hunt them down.

It was against the law for anyone to help runaways and masters had the right to search one another's property looking for fugitives. Recaptured slaves were branded FUG, for 'fugitive', on their foreheads or forced to wear iron collars inscribed with instructions to return them if they escaped again — just like a dog tag.

Verdict: TRUTH

Romans could sell themselves into slavery

The life of a slave in Ancient Rome was no fun at all. You might be made to work on a farm, or down a mine, or, if you were REALLY unfortunate, as a gladiator. Surely this wasn't a life you'd choose voluntarily?! Things would have to be really bad...

★ And the truth is...

Around a quarter of the people in the Roman Empire were slaves. Many were prisoners captured during Rome's wars of conquest, while others were traded from outside the empire.

Romans in debt could sell themselves to raise money and some criminals were sold into slavery as a punishment. In hard times the poor even sold their own kids into slavery.

Romans bought new slaves at special markets or from one another. Slaves were auctioned naked, so buyers could assess their health and fitness. *Tituli*, small labels, hung around their necks listing any special qualities or problems like: *Educated Greek – make good teacher* or *Boy from Britain, hard to train.*

Verdict: _____ TRUTH _____

Roman slaves stashed their cash

Slaves are not commonly associated with hordes of treasure, or, in fact, any treasure at all. We've been led to believe the life of a slave was all misery and drudgery. Was there some gold in it somewhere after all?

And the truth is...

Not all owners were cruel. Some masters believed slaves would work harder if they were treated fairly. Others came to like, or even love, their slaves and married them or adopted their children as their own.

Clever slaves were allowed to run businesses for their owners and save up to buy their freedom. This stash of cash was called a *peculium*. Other slaves were freed in their masters' wills as a reward for loyalty or hard work.

One famous example is Tiro, the slave of the politician Cicero. Tiro became his trusted secretary and continued to work for Cicero when he was freed. He lived to the age of 99 and earned enough money to buy a farm of his own — with slaves.

Verdict:

ROTTEN ROMANS

Vedius Pollio

Vedius Pollio was a powerful friend of the Emperor Augustus – and one of the cruellest slave owners in the Empire. His slaves were terrified of him, and with good reason. He kept fish – vampire fish.

Vedius's choice of aquatic pet was the lamprey. This charming creature feeds by latching on to prey with a huge, sucking mouth. Its barbed tongue opens a wound while it spits in anti-coagulants, which stop blood from clotting. And then it sucks the victim's blood.

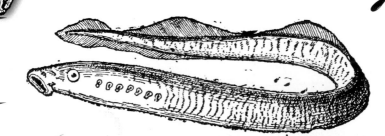

And yep, disgusting as it sounds, Vedius executed slaves who annoyed him by plunging them into a pool of lampreys. Death was slow and painful.

But Vedius got his comeuppance. He was entertaining Augustus at a banquet when a slave boy dropped and smashed a valuable crystal glass. Vedi was furious and ordered the poor lad be thrown to the lampreys.

Then the unexpected happened. The boy threw himself at the feet of the Emperor and begged to be killed cleanly — not to meet a messy end as fish food.

Augustus knew about his friend's nasty reputation but he was shocked that Vedius could act so cruelly while he was present. It was an insult to the emperor. Time to teach him who ruled Rome!

Augustus ordered that all of Vedius's best glasses be fetched by slaves — and smashed. The lamprey tank was filled in and the boy set free. And Augustus gained a reputation for mercy and good judgement. Nice one!

Rampaging Romans

The Spartacus Rebellion

Spartacus was a slave forced to train as a gladiator. In 73 BCE, he led a breakout of around 70 gladiators – armed only with kitchen tools! The fugitives set up a base near Mount Vesuvius and recruited an army of  resentful slaves, eager to fight for their freedom. Roman historians claimed that Spartacus led 70,000 men by the spring of 72 BCE.

It took eight Roman legions commanded by General Crassus (read about his sticky end on page 18) to hunt the slave army down. Most were killed in battles, but 6,000 were crucified along the Appian Way. Spartacus's body was never identified.

The Romans watched executions for fun

Romans believed that criminals such as murderers or bandits deserved to die painful and brutal deaths. But did they really enjoy WATCHING this happen?

★ And the truth is...

The Romans enjoyed savage sports in amphitheatres across the Empire. The most famous amphitheatre was the Colosseum in Rome, but many towns, such as Deva Victrix (Chester) in Britain, had smaller versions. The arena was a sandy floor that soaked up the blood of the victims.

Part of the thrill was watching the execution of criminals — by crucifixion, burning alive or perhaps being hunted down by fellow prisoners in desperate fights — but this was simply the lunchtime filler.

The warm-up acts were beast fights — perhaps a pack of dogs set on a lion or an enraged elephant trampling armoured hunters. To keep the crowd in their seats, the best came last — the gladiators.

A typical fight pitted a *retiarius* (no armour, net and trident) against a *secutor* (armour, short sword and shield). They fought until one gladiator was defeated, wounded or killed.

Verdict: TRUTH

GRUESOME

To keep things interesting in the arena, the Romans trained lots of different kinds of gladiators. Here's a one-stop guide to the most common so, should you ever find yourself at some gladiatorial games, you'll be able to identify who's who:

SECUTOR

RETIARUS

GLADIATORS

Bestiarus — the *bestiarii*, as their name suggests, fought wild beasts, usually lions or bears.

Cestus — the *cestuses* were boxers who wore *cestuses*, a nastier version of modern boxing gloves. Cestuses were made of strips of leather, and sometimes included iron plates, blades or spikes.

Dimachaerus — the *dimachaeri* fought with two swords: one in each hand. They were highly skilled close-combat fighters, and greatly respected in the gladiatorial world.

Eques — the *equites* began their fights on horseback, but after they had thrown their lance, they dismounted and fought on foot using short swords.

Essedarius — the *essedarii* fought from chariots, charging at their opponents and either running them down or impaling them on their spear.

Murmillo — the *murmillones* were heavily armed gladiators, who wore helmets, arm and shin guards and thick leather belts, and carried shields and short swords. All the armour made them quite slow, and they were often pitted against faster, more lightly armed gladiators.

Retiarus — the *retiarii* fought with weapons suitable for a fisherman: a weighted net, a three-pointed trident and a dagger. The retiarii made up for their lack of heavy weaponry by being fast, agile, and light on their feet.

Scissor — the *scissores* carried a short sword with two blades, which looked like a pair of open scissors.

Secutor — *secutores* were developed to fight the retiarii. They were armed in a similar fashion to the murmillones, but their helmets covered their entire faces, with just two small eyeholes, to protect against the retiarii's tridents.

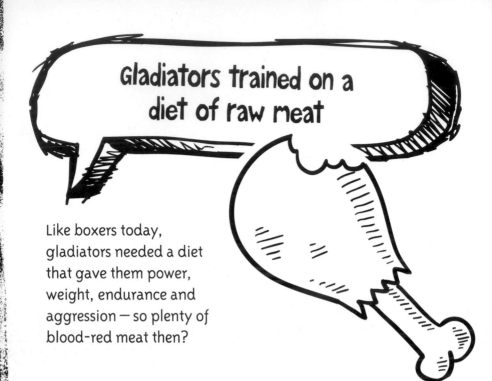

Gladiators trained on a diet of raw meat

Like boxers today, gladiators needed a diet that gave them power, weight, endurance and aggression — so plenty of blood-red meat then?

 And the truth is...

Well, no. A steak diet is high in protein, and boxers actually need carbohydrates, for energy. A typical diet plan for a modern boxer recommends plenty of wholegrain breads and pasta, brown rice and sweet potatoes.

The ancient equivalent of this was... beans. Gladiators fed on a gruel called *sagina* made from beans and barley. This gave them plenty of muscle and bulk. They ate so much sagina they were sometimes called *hordearii* or 'barleymen'.

Verdict: — **BUSTED** —

Warm gladiator blood was used as medicine

Headline News: A top footballer breaks his nose and bleeds on the goal line. Suddenly excited fans pour on to the pitch and wipe up the drops. Sounds pretty mad! Was this everyday behaviour for fans of the gladiatorial arena?

★ And the truth is...

Guys stepped aside and girls swooned when top gladiators walked by. They were stars and their devotees believed that gladiator blood was magic — the fresher the better.

New brides had their hair parted with a spear dipped in gladiator's blood to help them become pregnant, while the medical writer Celsus commented:

Some have freed themselves from epilepsy by drinking deep drafts of the warm blood from a gladiator's throat.

Even the blood-stained sand was used in love potions.

Verdict: **TRUTH**

Roman women were banned from the arena

Remember Juvenal, the moaning poet (pages 37 and 39)? Another of his gripes was about female gladiators:

Who has not seen the dummies of wood they slash at
Whether with swords or with spears?
Are they really preparing for the arena? How can a woman be decent
Sticking her head in a helmet, denying the sex she was born with?

⭐ And the truth is...

Despite the grumblers, some women did become successful gladiators. A carving from Turkey shows two *gladiatrices* fighting one another. We even know their arena names — *Amazon* and *Achilla*. Remarkably they fought in full armour, weighing at least 15 kilograms — so these were two tough gals. The inscription states they slugged it out to an honourable draw.

Archaeologists believe they found the grave of a professional *gladiatrix* in Southwark in 1996. She fought in the arena in Londinium in front of crowds of up to 7,000 people. The woman died in her early 20s and was given an elaborate and expensive funeral.

Verdict: ── **BUSTED** ──

Games fans were as violent as gladiators

Ancient crowds could be as violent as any modern football mob — and they were armed with swords!! But surely they weren't as violent as the men or women fighting to the death in front of them?

★ And the truth is...

In 59 CE, a riot broke out at the gladiator games in Pompeii. The locals started fighting with the visiting spectators from nearby Nuceria. Taunts led to stone throwing, and stone throwing led to swords being drawn...

It was carnage: parents and children were killed, and the wounded had to be carried as far as Rome (more than 240 kilometres away) for treatment. Pompeii was banned from staging games for ten years, and the leading rioters were sent into exile.

Verdict: ——— **TRUTH** ———

Roman charioteers earned superstar wages

The top modern sporting heroes earn
superstar wages, making them
millionaires many times over. But
could Roman athletes dream of
such riches?

And the truth is...

A massive YES, some Roman sports stars were paid a FORTUNE.

The best paid of all Roman athletes were charioteers, the star drivers of the fastest sport in the Empire. Charioteers worked for teams backed by businessmen — a bit like Formula 1 racing today. There were usually four race teams: Red, White, Blue and Green, each with gangs of diehard fans.

Drivers wore a leather helmet, shin guards, a chest protector and a jersey in the team colours. They carried a whip, and a curved knife — handy for cutting the reins of opponents who got too close.

The emperor started the races by dropping a napkin, then a mounted umpire tried to keep order. After seven savage laps, the first three drivers won prizes. Crashes and deaths thrilled the crowds to fever pitch and fights amongst fans were common.

Verdict:

TRUTH

ROTTEN ROMANS

Gaius Appuleius Diocles

The most famous Roman charioteer was Gaius Appuleius Diocles from Hispania (modern Spain), who lived during the 2nd century CE. Gaius' speciality was the superfast four-horse chariot. His career began with the White Team when he was 18, but his greatest success came when he joined the Red Team at the age of 27.

In 24 action-packed years he scored 1,462 wins and earned a fortune – his prize money added up to a breathtaking 35,863,120 sesterces, about £9.6 billion (or US$15 billion) in today's money. That was enough to pay for the whole Roman army for two months, or the grain supply for the city of Rome for a year. Juvenal moaned (what a surprise) that he was better paid than the richest Senator.

Gaius retired at the age of 42, also impressive in a sport where many competitors died young.

Romans went speed-dating at the chariot racing

The Circus Maximus was the beating heart of the Empire — the vast sports stadium filled up with 150,000 people for the weekly chariot races. But did the Romans really use it for more than watching the racing?

⭐ And the truth is...

100% yes. Young people gathered at the Circus Maximus to meet. Rich girls escorted by chaperones could slip away in the crowds.

Young men followed the advice of the poet Ovid: Sit close to a girl and plump up her cushion. Offer her a stool for her feet and make sure no-one in the row behind sticks their knees into her back.

Ovid even suggests a 'get to know you' line: *I wish you looked at me like you do at that charioteer.*

Verdict: _____

The Romans celebrated Valentine's Day with goatskin whips

Think Valentine's Day, think cards, flowers and chocolates. BORING. Did the Romans have more fun?

 And the truth is...

On 15 February, the Romans celebrated Lupercalia, an ancient festival even in Roman times. Roman men sacrificed goats or dogs, skinned them and made whips from their hides. Daubed in blood, they ran naked round the streets, whacking any women they came across.

Far from hiding, young women joined in, lining up to be hit. They believed the whips would help them to have children. And of course there was lots of drunkenness and feasting. No wonder Lupercalia was a favourite Roman festival! The dates are just a coincidence though, Lupercalia was a spring festival, not linked to Valentine's Day.

Verdict:

The Romans were awed by the supernatural

Very practical people the Romans — great builders and even better fighters. But aqueducts and armies couldn't control the gods and fate. So how did they keep on the right side of supernatural powers?

⭐ And the truth is...

Omens were a way of trying to predict the future. Ordinary people kept an eye open for bad omens in everyday life: a black cat in the house, a snake falling from a tree, spilling wine or olive oil were all signs that something nasty might happen.

The Roman state took omens seriously too. A general would not fight a battle or the Senate make a big decision before a seer had taken the omens. A seer was a wise man who looked at the entrails (guts) of a sacrificed animal or watched scared chickens feed.

If the entrails were rotten or the chickens refused to eat, it was time to do... nothing. Try again another, luckier day.

Verdict:

GOOD GOD!

Are you baffled by Bacchus? Mystified by Minerva? Worry not! Follow our bit-by-bit guide to some members of the Holy Roman Family:

MINERVA

The daughter of Jupiter, and the Roman goddess of music, poetry, craft, magic and wisdom, among other things. Phew! Busy lady. Minerva is often depicted with an owl, symbolising wisdom. She was the half-sister of...

MERCURY

The messenger god, and the son of Jupiter and Maia, the goddess of growth. The element mercury is named after him, because it is volatile and changes quickly, just as the god Mercury moved at speed from place to place. Mercury was also supposed to guide the souls of dead people to the Underworld, where Romans believed they went after death.

The Romans would have loved Harry Potter

What did the Romans make of wizards and spells?
Would Harry Potter have been a top-selling scroll
if J. K. Rowlingus had been a Roman author? And
where would Hogwarts have been?

And the truth is...

The Romans turned to witches, wizards and sorcerers
of all kinds for help in hard times. And they paid good
money for the right spell or potion.

The Romans believed the best magic training and the finest
wizards came from Egypt. Trainee wizards studied ancient
magical *papyri*, or documents.

Hundreds of pages gave detailed instructions like:
*When you are about to use the lamp of divination first put an
ointment in your eyes. This shall be made from some flowers of
the Greek bean.*

To impress clients, wizards had magic kits that included roulette
wheels for telling the future, wands for directing power and
incense to create the right atmosphere for a consultation.

Verdict:

Romans were spooked by their own dreams

Dreams can be terrifying sometimes (particularly if you've been snacking on cheese before bed) but we all know they're just that, right? Only a dream. Were the Romans really frightened of their own night-time imaginings?

⭐ And the truth is...

The Romans believed dreams needed to be explained and turned to the wily Greek Artemidorus Ephesius for guidance. Arty wrote the *Oneirocritica (The Interpretation of Dreams)* in the 2nd century and all the best libraries kept a copy. Modern historians use it as evidence for the day-to-day worries of ordinary Romans.

Some of Artemidorus' explanations were scary though:

Dream: You can't find your way out of your own house.

Interpretation: You are about to catch a serious disease or die.

And some more encouraging:

Dream: You have a large head.

Interpretation: If you are rich you will become a leader, if you are poor you will find success.

Verdict:

GOOD GOD!

Are you baffled by Bacchus? Mystified by Minerva? Worry not! Follow our bit-by-bit guide to some members of the Holy Roman Family:

VENUS

The goddess of love, beauty, fertility and prosperity, Venus was also the wife of Vulcan and the mother of Cupid. The month of April was dedicated to her, and on 1 April, the Romans celebrated the festival of the Veneralia in her honour. During this festival, her statue was taken from its temple in Rome, carried to the men's baths, washed in warm water and garlanded with myrtle, an evergreen plant. Roman men and women would then ask Venus for help in affairs of the heart.

BACCHUS

The god of the grape harvest, wine and winemaking, Bacchus is often shown holding a staff called a thyrsus and bunches of grapes. The Romans held festivals called Bacchanalia in Bacchus' honour. Unsurprisingly, these were raucous affairs, and in 186 CE the Roman Senate intervened in an attempt to control their size and organisation.

93

Where can I find myths about...

amphitheatres 63, 77
animals 5, 13, 16, 18, 19, 21, 23, 28, 29, 31, 34, 35, 36, 47, 51, 57, 59, 60, 61, 68, 77, 79, 88, 89
astrology 44-45

banquets 10, 62
baths 40-41, 42-43, 64-65
Britain 7, 19, 21, 25, 29, 37, 72, 77

chariots 22, 35, 38, 51, 79, 84-85, 86, 87
children 20, 48-49, 50, 53, 54, 71, 72, 73, 83
Circus Maximus, the 38, 87
clothes 10, 20, 21, 49, 51, 82, 85
Colosseum, the 38, 63, 77
criminals 21, 44-45, 72, 77
crucifixion 13, 23, 59, 76, 77

disease 26, 65

emperors 5, 16, 37, 40, 68
  Augustus (Octavian) 6, 16, 17, 33, 44, 54-56
  Britannicus 16, 58-59
  Caesar 7, 14-15, 17, 19, 33
  Caligula 5, 16, 17, 20, 21
  Claudius 7, 16, 17, 19, 58
  Constantine 7, 49
  Diocletian 40

Elagabalus 46
Hadrian 7, 25
Marcus Aurelius 26, 65
Nepos, Julius 7
Nero 16, 17, 22-23, 58-59, 61
Tiberius 16, 17
Trajan 7, 12

festivals 10, 47, 88
food 23, 29, 43, 49, 56, 58, 59, 60, 61, 62, 70, 80
Forum, the 38
games 43, 50, 83
generals 14, 18, 20, 28, 33, 76, 89
gladiators 5, 6, 21, 27, 76, 77, 78-79, 80, 81, 82, 83
gods and goddesses
  Apollo 51
  Diana 51
  Mars 5, 30, 47
  Juno 30, 47
  Jupiter 10, 30, 47, 51, 90
  Mercury 90
  Minerva 10, 30, 47, 51, 90
  Neptune 10
  Pluto 10
  Saturn 10, 30
  Venus 21
  Vulcan 30, 47

honestiores and
  humiliores 12-13
hunting 19, 51, 77

Latin 5, 8-9
laws 13, 71
legions 12, 18, 25, 29, 31, 76

magic 91
medicine 5, 27, 46, 81
money 19, 72, 73, 84, 86

omens 89

plague 7, 26
poison 16, 56, 58
Pompeii 7, 67, 83
postal service 68

roads 4, 68, 69
Rome 5, 6, 8, 9, 13, 14, 21, 22-23, 26, 37, 38, 39, 40, 44, 61, 77, 86

slaves 6, 10, 19, 39, 42, 44, 49, 62, 65, 70-71, 72, 73, 76
  Spartacus 6, 76
soldiers 5, 13, 19, 26, 28-29, 31, 35, 47, 49

taxes 44
torture 13, 70

wars 6, 14, 15, 16, 18, 33, 47, 54, 72, 76
weapons 29, 31, 32, 36, 77, 79, 82, 83, 85
women 53, 54-56, 71, 82, 83

100%
SUCKER-PROOF

GUARANTEED!

Take a look at our other marvellously mythbusting titles...

Tip:
Turn over!

PHEW!
eh?
hortle
check it out!
Really?
WOW!
tee-hee!
That's incredible!
I can't believe it!
You're pulling my leg
FREAKY!
COR!
No way!
ell, I ever!
It's Amazing!
Awesome!